Disclosure

I have changed the names of some of the people in this book to protect their identity. Reading this book does not guarantee success in any business. It does not guarantee you will make money. This book is simply a guideline to help guide you in the right direction to creating a bigger, better, brighter future for yourself and your family. To be truly successful, become financially free, and get out of the "Rat Race" will take hard work, determination, and an iron will, that this book cannot provide. It is up to you as the reader to take the information from this book and apply it to your everyday life, your business, and your family. This book will help you understand how the Wealthy think, along with some of the secrets they hold.

The only way to become successful is to want it. To want it more than you want air.

A Little About Me

In this book I will teach you some of the secrets the wealthy do not want you to know. I will give you the information you need to help pave the way to a better financial future. I would like to tell everyone reading this book however; Financial freedom is not easily obtained. You will have to work hard. Harder than you've ever worked before. You will be tested, physically, emotionally, and mentally. But once you reach that final stretch; Once you fire your boss; Once you never have to worry about how you're going to pay your bills, or feed your family, you will realize just how worth it, it really is.

I'm going to start off by telling you a little about myself. They say you only take advice from people you know, like and trust. That's exactly what I want to accomplish in this first chapter. I want you to be able to understand who I am as a person, some of the hardships I have gone through, to see what may lie ahead in your journey to financial freedom, but most importantly I want you to feel as though you can take my advice, learn from it, and change your life for the better. I don't want this to be another one of those books you buy because you think it will help you start a business, make more money, or better your life, but it not do just that. There have been many books I've bought throughout the years, hoping it will somehow impact my life in a positive way, but in reality they all said the same thing; and most of what they said I'd read in every other book of the same genre. I truly hope this isn't just another one of those books for you.

As you can see by the cover of this book, my name is Jacob Moore. What you can't see is that I am an entrepreneur; business owner, real estate investor, father, and family man. My story starts when I was seventeen years old in the town of Saint Joseph Missouri. At seventeen years old I was a senior in high school. Throughout most of my life I wanted to be many different things when I grew up. A teacher, policeman, firefighter, but it wasn't until my senior year of high school when reality set in and I knew I had to find a career that I would be happy in soon, or I was doomed to go from job to job, destined to be unhappy with true adulthood before it ever really started. Now I was never the smartest kid in school, I would often skip classes and when I did show up to call most people only knew it was me by the back of my head. Yes, I slept a lot in school. I always managed to get good grades, but not good enough to get me into college on any scholarships. My family not having a lot of money at the time I knew college wasn't going to be in my future.

Because we didn't have the money to send me to college and I wasn't going to get any scholarships I decided to do the one thing I knew I was going to be able to do and still get some kind of college education. I joined the military. May of 2011 it was official. I was a Military Police Officer in the United States Army.

I must admit, I wasn't in the military very long, and I do miss it from time to time. But after serving a brief period in the Army, life wanted to take me in another direction. Once I was home, a typical civilian, I thought as most young adults do, the world was in the palm of my hand, there wasn't anything I couldn't do. After all I learned everything I would ever need to know from my time in the Army. Or so I thought. I quickly learned just how difficult it was to find a career, let alone a job alone.

My parents were always fairly strict on us kids. But they were always fair. They would tell us growing up, after high school we had Three choices, go to college, join the military, or get out of their house. A lesson I always thought to be very harsh, but now that I see the importance of the lesson they were trying to teach us I'm very grateful for.

Once I was a civilian again my parents offered to let me live with them again, they gave me back my old bedroom, which at that point was my dad's office, and they set some guidelines. The most important being, I had six months to find a job and move out. Me being young and dumb I thought that was awesome. It was going to be so easy for me to get a job, especially a nice high paying one. I mean I knew everything there was to know after all. Or so I thought like most young adults that age do.

I quickly spent through the money I had managed to save while I was in the Army, nothing too big, just a few thousand dollars. But it wasn't until I was flat broke and without a job that I realized just how easy it was to save that few thousand dollars, while living on base in Fort Leonard Wood Missouri, which meant, not paying utilities, to buying groceries, paying for internet, or any of the things I had grown accustomed to. With no money, no job, and just a few short months to move out I finally decided it was time for me to find a job. My first real job after high school. It took about a month for me to finally get an interview at a temp service in town. The temp service was looking for machine operators for a factory in town.

The interview went well and within a few short weeks I had finally gotten a job. This job paid somewhere in the neighborhood of

Fourteen dollars an hour. Which to me was great, that came out to about what I was making in the military, plus I knew after I was hired full time I would get a pay raise of about Three dollars more. I was excited to say the least.

It only took about a month after starting my new job that I moved out. Even though my parents had a nice big house that I could have lived in for just a few more months, I knew it was time for me to move on with my life and start acting like an adult. It was definitely scary, signing a year lease for an apartment, especially one that was as small as this one. That in itself was terrifying. But I learned to embrace the suck, and that is exactly what I did.

I worked at this factory for a couple of years, I really enjoyed it. Even though I worked in a freezer Ten to Twelve hours a day, my body grew accustomed to the below freezing temp, I worked extra hard to help produce a little extra body heat and I made some great lifelong friends. To this day it is still one of my favorite places I've ever worked. Throughout the few years I worked there, I focused on progressing higher up the chain. Moving up to higher paying jobs, even applying for management positions. Once I got as high as I could possibly go without the right college education needed to go higher up the chain, I started looking for a new job.

Obviously I loved my job, I enjoyed the staff that I worked with on a daily basis, and I knew that I would miss my job, but that's part of life. Everyone wants to "keep up with the joneses" and I knew I wasn't going to be able to do that at that particular job. I wanted nicer things, a nicer car, bigger apartment, eventually a house. That being said I was very picky about the new jobs I started applying for. They had to pay more than what I was making, and they had to be first shift jobs.

Eventually I found one at another factory making pet food. It wasn't a guaranteed first shift job, but it paid three dollars more an hour then I was making, and eventually when there was an opening on first shift I knew I could try to get it. Instead I was stuck being a floater. I went where I was needed, between all three shifts, and every line they could get me trained on.

The first few months were fantastic. Soon I was living in one of the nicest apartments I'd ever seen, I had a nice car, it wasn't brand new, but it was pretty dang close. I was finally able to keep up with the joneses. What I didn't know, and what I definitely wasn't ready for was the reality of being a floater after you finish your initial orientation training period. Once I finished orientation is when my life came crumbling down on top of me. I never realized how many people the average workplace is missing each and every day until I had to cover for them. Twelve hour days, five days a week, and often not on the same shift for more than Two days was now my normal work schedule. It went on like this for months. I wasn't able to sleep because of the odd hours and never being on the same shift for long, my body wasn't given the appropriate time to get used to a sleep schedule, making it very difficult to sleep, eat, or even function on a daily basis.

This went on until one day at work I fell asleep, and not only did I just fall asleep at work, I actually fell asleep standing up, while I was working. A manager of mine quickly saw what was happening and a few days later I was let go.

The obviously thing to do in a situation like this, is to hurry and find a new job, preferably one that can sustain the lifestyle that you're living. The grown up thing to do, is find a job, any job that can pay your bills and put food on the table. I didn't do either one of these. Instead I had the great idea to take a few weeks off from working. In my head I had just left a job that used up all of my time and I had plenty of money in savings to take a few weeks off work.

That was the best worst mistake of my life. Having had a steady job for a few years only to transfer from one job to the next I had underestimated how difficult it still was to find a job, especially one that paid as much as my last one. Within Three weeks I was in debt, I hadn't even bothered applying for unemployment when I was fired because I was sure it would be easy for me to find a new job and partly because I was ashamed to admit that I was fired for falling asleep on the job.

It wasn't long before I stopped paying all of my bills. I just couldn't afford it. I had too much pride to apply for something like food stamps, so once I finally decided to apply for unemployment and was granted a check for a few hundred dollars a month, I spent all of my money on food. Not only food, I must admit I slipped into alcoholism. Looking back, I probably had more beer in my fridge then I did food.

Still without a job, eventually my landlord became concerned about why I wasn't paying my rent, and why I was months behind. I tried everything I could to avoid her until I came up with enough money to pay her what was owed. Which was very difficult seeing as how my bank account was closed due to being hundreds of dollars in the hole. So I did what I feel anyone would do in this situation, I started selling things. My cell phone was turned off due to owing the phone company over One Thousand dollars, so I sold the phone that I had on that plan. I also sold my tablet, a laptop, my brand new game systems, I sold everything I thought would be of some sort of value. Yes, even my Sixty-Five-inch tv my parents gave me. But even then after selling all of that stuff, everything I'd worked so hard for, I still didn't have enough to pay all of the money I owed.

That's where my story really begins.

Still jobless, living off just over Two Hundred dollars a week of unemployment I knew I had to do something to earn some extra money. That's when my first business was started. Hero's Personal Training. I've always been very fond of going to the gym. Pushing myself physically as far as I could go. So I took that passion that I had and created my first business out of it. The only issue was, I didn't know how to run a business.

Hero's Personal Training didn't last very long. I didn't have the marketing skills to let people know there was a new personal trainer in town. I didn't have the knowledge to know how much to charge people for each session. Or if I should even charge them for each session versus charging them for an entire month's crash training course. Needless to say I was desperate. So desperate I offered anyone who was willing to give me a chance a free weeks worth of training. That was great, until no one came back for week number Two.

It wasn't until I was completely broken, driving my life deeper and deeper into a dark abyss I wasn't sure I would ever get out of that I found it.

While scrolling through Craigslist still searching for a job I came across an ad that caught my attention. The subject line read something along the lines of "Real Estate Investor Seeks Apprentice Earn $120K per Year Part Time."

Now that caught my attention. Something I could do part time and earn Three times as much money as I was before. It had to be too good to be true. But I sent in my resume anyway. The worst thing that would happen would be me not qualifying for the position.

Within a few days I was reached out to by an amazing woman, someone I'm still close friends with even to this day. She asked me a few questions about my personal life and why I wanted to be a Real Estate Investor, normal questions you would be asked at any interview. Then she set me up on a live webinar with her team's leader. It only took Fifteen minutes before I was convinced this man was the smartest man I'd ever heard talk. He was a genius. He was the very first person to ever explain to me that I was what is called an entrepreneur. I'd never heard that word before, but everything he said resonated within me. When he described to me what exactly an entrepreneur is it sounded like he was describing me almost perfectly.

After a couple times meeting with this group of Real Estate Investors over a webinar platform they hit me with the bombshell I knew was coming. They weren't just training anyone to be Real Estate Investors; and definitely not for free. What this group did was sell online classes that taught Real Estate Investing and Business. Classes ranged from Two Thousand dollars to Twenty Thousand dollars. Way outside of my budget.

I kept in touch with this group for about a year. By that time, I had found a new job, gotten a new apartment, and caught up on most of my debt. I was finally ready to commit to furthering my education. By that time, I had found a new family, a beautiful wife who just so happened to have an amazing little boy, and was now carrying my very first child. I knew it was time to do something with my life, something that was going to affect my new family's life in the most positive way possible. They deserved it.

Secret Number 1

A Powerful Why

You've probably heard this One Hundred times over, and I never knew the significance of it, until I did. But it's like a good friend of mine says "You don't know what you don't know."

Your why is everything in your business. It's your driving force, your motivation, your reason for working Eighty hour weeks without complaint. It doesn't matter what your why is; whether it be for your family, for financial freedom, or just to be your own boss. What your "why" is, doesn't matter as long as that why is strong enough.

As I said, it has to be strong enough to motivate you to work Eighty hour weeks, even if you don't make any money for the first few months. Even the first year. If your why is powerful enough, you'll succeed. That I promise.

My "why" is my family. As I said before, at one point in my life I had slipped into a deep dark abyss that I thought was impossible to escape. It wasn't until I met my wife and my step son that I knew I could escape. I could escape and I could thrive. They were the driving force to changing my life. Because of that they deserve everything I can ever give them. I don't want my kids to have to live through that same situation. Jobless, Homeless, and without hope. These are all things I hope none of you ever have to go through. And I have and still to this day I am, fighting as hard as I can to create a life and a business that will never allow my kids to be forced to go through something like that.

Creating a business, especially a successful one takes time. It takes time, patience and determination. When I first started my business I went over a year and a half without making a single dime. I made no money but spent several hundreds of dollars in an attempt to be successful. But I never gave up, I never gave up because I have the strongest "why" possible. My kids, my family, their future.

Many people often have a very strong why, but still fail in their attempts to create successful businesses. This is because over the weeks, months, years of trying but failing they lose sight of that "why" factor.

In an attempt to combat this, I have a few suggestions on how you can always remember your "why" and never let it fail.

You can start by writing your "why" down on sticky notes and plastering them all over your home. Put one on the bathroom mirror. Putting a sticky note with your "why" on it, on your bathroom mirror is a daily reminder for you why you're doing what you're doing. Every time you brush your teeth, comb your hair, shave your face, pluck your eyebrows; whatever the case is. Every time you look into that mirror you will be reminded.

I would also suggest taking a picture of your "why" on your phone or tablet. Take a picture of it and set it as your background. Now every time you look at your phone you'll be reminded.

You can also place sticky notes on your refrigerator, computer, anywhere that you look on a daily basis, put one there. If your "why" is your family, tell them so they can remind you every day how grateful they are that you're doing this for them.

Whatever you do and however you do it, just make sure you are reminded every day why you're working so hard.

Diamonds aren't made overnight, yet they're one of the most valuable rock on earth.

One of the most difficult challenges you'll face in your first year is, the overwhelming feeling of failure, defeat. Or the sense of wanting to give up. These feelings may not even originate in your own mind. When you first start out in whatever business you're planning to create many people, friends, family, loved ones, some of them will tell you things such as,

"You can't do this."

"You're not smart enough."

"You don't know what you're doing."

"You're wasting your time."

"You'll never succeed in that business."

They may be right. But that's up to you. Again this all comes back to your "why". If your "why" is powerful enough you cannot fail. If your "why" is powerful enough to won't accept anything less than complete success.

When people say things like this, these negative comments, it's because they don't understand the power of human emotion.

It's been said throughout history that human emotion is the most powerful tool we have, and in starting your own business, that saying stands strong.

Recap

To be successful in any business you need a powerful "Why" factor. Again what your "Why" is doesn't matter, all that matters is this "why" is powerful enough to motivate you to do the hard work necessary and it needs to be a powerful driving force on your road to success.

Before you move to the next chapter I want you to stop and think.

I want you to think of why you want to be a successful business professional. Is it for your family? If it is, why do you want to be a success for them?

When you're thinking about what your "why" factor is, I want you to question why, that is your "why".

Secret Number 2

You Don't Know What You Don't Know

A good friend of mine Bill, told me this a few years ago. He said "You don't know what you don't know." Something so simple yet so very true. Sometimes I think it's so simple in fact that many people overlook it.

If there is anything I want you to take from this book it's this, your "Why" factor will make you a success if it's powerful enough. But just because you become a success doesn't mean you will stay successful. You must always be training your brain, educating yourself, and studying not only your business, but everything you can.

Knowledge is power, we've all heard that before. But what most people don't understand is all of the different things you must be knowledgeable in to run a single successful business.

I want to use myself as an example, my most prominent business is in Real Estate. I am a Real Estate Investor. But to be a successful Real Estate Investor I have to be knowledgeable in multiple different subjects. Tax and Legal, Marketing, Problem Solving, Creative Solutions, Sales, Finances, Management, and that's not even close to being it. I have to know multiple different exit strategies, Wholesale, Short Sale, Fix and Flip, Buy and Hold, Notes, Probate, Seller Finance, Master Lease Options, Deeds, I need to know what a mortgage is, how to create an all-star team. There are so many different subjects I must be familiar with to be successful in the Real Estate market.

Not only do I need to consistently study all of these subjects but I also need to keep up on market trends for the areas I purchase real estate in, I need to keep up to date on all of the laws and regulations in these areas in case a law changes. I need to be able to tell if the market is going up or coming down and how to prepare myself for that situation.

There is so much you need to learn about any business you want to get involved in that you will never learn all of it. So start now, it doesn't matter how you study just as long as you are constantly learning new things that pertain to your business or the things involved with your business. I don't care if you pay people to teach you these things or you learn them at the library or on YouTube. Learning is what's important here.

Now, you do have to be careful, there are plenty of people out in the world as sad as it is, that will charge you money to teach you something outdated that will only hinder your business. So please be careful.

Please remember to take everything you learn with a grain of salt. And don't think just because someone said it's going to work it will, even if it worked for them. We're all different, we all have different needs, expectations, experiences, and even marketplaces. For example, in Texas it is illegal to buy real estate with a rent to own agreement. But in Missouri it's not. So if I live in Texas and I'm new to real estate investing and I'm taking advice from someone who specializes in rent to own real estate deals, that person is probably going to tell me to start off doing what? Renting to own properties. But the first time I do that I've broken the law, but being new to real estate investing I might not know that.

So you see, you need to study and learn as much as you possibly can, but you also need to make sure you're getting your facts from a credible source. What I would suggest is getting a mentor. A mentor is an amazing thing no matter what business you're in for a few different reasons.

1. This mentor is most likely already successful in the business field you're interested in.
2. This mentor has more than likely already went to the school of hard knock and can save you a trip there yourself.
3. Depending on what your agreement is for this mentor you may be just as big of an asset to him as he is to you.

Think of it this way. If you are interested in being a Real Estate Investor and you find a successful Investor to be your mentor. Maybe you come to some sort of agreement as to where he teaches you how to invest in real estate, maybe he gives you the cash for your very first deal, but you have to do all the work on the deal yourself, even though he's there to answer any questions you have, you do all of the work, and he gets maybe Seventy percent of the commission that comes from your first deal. Or maybe you just start investing for him, he teaches you the ropes, you invest his money for him and he keeps all of the money until you start investing for yourself. Either one of these scenarios your mentor is going to teach you everything he can about Real Estate Investing because you're using his money and he's making a profit, even though he's not doing any work.

In this day and age there are literally thousands of ways you can study and learn any subject you please. It doesn't matter how you study as long as you continue to study. And for those of you who don't like to study, I'm sorry but if you want to truly be a success and stay a success you will most likely be studying until the day you retire. But if you're passionate about your business, whether you like to study or not you I can almost guarantee, once you start learning all these new things you'll continue to study well past retirement.

Recap

"You don't know what you don't know." That sentence says so much in just a few words. Knowledge is power and much like a light bulb needs a consistent flow of electricity to keep itself on and bright, your business is going to need a consistent flow of information and knowledge coming in to thrive in the ever changing world we live in.

To have a successful business your business must be able to adapt where it's needed and when. The best way to do that is to have the knowledge to see when the changes are coming and how you can adapt to fit its needs.

Simple Systems

Yes, you read that right. The Third secret is simple systems. Many young entrepreneurs think that to be a great business owner you must have these complex systems and that just isn't the case. The best systems are ones that can be duplicated and ran to be just as effective by someone who doesn't know anything about the system itself. The military had a saying I think pertains very well to creating systems. K.I.S.S or Keep It Simple Stupid.

Simplicity in itself makes everything easier, so why go out and create a complex system? Think of it this way, the more moving parts your money has to go through, the more money is going to fall off. It won't be anyone's fault; it's just the way complex systems are.

I've never understood why people create complex systems. But I do have to hand it to them, at least they made a system.

I want to take a second and explain to you what a system is and why it's important to have systems in the first place.

A system to me is an automated routine that happens within your business that generates you positive cash flow or some form of result that will bring you a positive cash flow. For example, a system I have in my real estate business is an application that automatically sends me an email when a property matching a certain description goes up for sale on specific websites. And then from there the possible lead will go through multiple other systems before I ever touch it.

This not only helps automate my business but it also allows me to spend the time I would normally be working, with my family. I said in previous chapters that you will be faced with working Eighty hour weeks, well with the correct systems in place you could potentially fully automate your business and stop working those horrid hours. Spend more time with your family and friends, actually have a chance to live your life for once.

Now you do have to keep up with your systems, and by that I mean you must keep an eye on them, perform maintenance to them, update them, upgrade them, anything and everything you can to keep them running as smoothly and efficiently as possible.

And don't be afraid to have more than one system in place, chances are you're going to need multiple systems that can work together, to even partially automate your business. I think that's where a lot of business owners mess up. They think they need these complex systems, or even worse, they pay a monthly fee for a system that's already set up and they have no idea how to use it. Then they realize they have to create Five more systems for this and that and everything becomes one big jumbled mess.

You want to get your money in the most simplistic way possible, I know you do, so do just that, create simple systems that work well together. Now not all of your systems will work out the way you want them to, some you'll scrap and need to start over with, some you will work really well for this or that, but they don't work well in conjunction with your other systems. It's going to be a trial and error type of deal and that's okay. What's important is that you're not creating systems that are too complex or confusing for you to handle. Again the best type of systems are the ones that can be duplicated and ran by someone who doesn't know anything about them.

But I must say, more importantly than having simple systems is having systems in general. Over the past few years I've met hundreds of people looking to start their first business, a lot of them were already working on their first business. But they didn't have any systems in place. Without systems you're are stuck doing all of the work. Meaning you will work Eight hour weeks until you give up because you're working too much. "Which isn't going to happen because you will have simple systems and a powerful "why" factor." Or you're going to retire. I even consider hiring an employee a system, because after their trained in how to do their jobs they will then be automating your business and bringing in positive cash flow.

Recap

Having good working systems that can work together to help automate your business are essential in taking that next step to becoming one of the wealthy. But using simple to use and simple to duplicate systems could potentially make or break your business.

I want you to take a second and ask yourself, would you rather work with Fifty different systems that are confusing and complex even for yourself. Or would you rather sit back on the beach with a cold drink making positive cash flow because you have such simple systems you hired someone and taught them to maintain, update, and run them? The choice is yours, but for me, the beach sounds pretty nice right about now.

Secret Number 4

Tax Deductions

I know what you're thinking, all business professionals know about tax deductions. While tax deductions are a no brainer to most business professionals, what the wealthy might not want you to know is just how much their writing off on their taxes, and more importantly What their writing off on their taxes.

For example, did you know you can write your kids off on your taxes? And no, I don't mean claiming them on your taxes for the benefit. You can actually write off your kids on your taxes as a tax deduction.

Imagine this: Owning a business in Real Estate Investing. Now imagine using pictures of your kids in your marketing campaign. Nothing fancy, just a nice picture of them playing in the backyard of a property you have for sale. Now because you're using your kids' picture in your marketing campaign you can pay your kids. Regardless of age, you're paying them for their service. To make it simple we'll say your kids are Sixteen years old and you're paying them One Hundred dollars for each picture. Now let's say you only take one picture, just to keep the math simple.

Now, you've paid your kids a crisp One-Hundred-dollar bill. Now let's say you have two kids. So that's Two Hundred dollars total, right? Now because your kids are on your payroll and you've paid them, that it now a business expense. Still following? Now the tax law says you can write off One Hundred percent of all business expenses. So you pay your kids Two hundred dollars in total, One Hundred each. You write it off as a business expense because they're on your business' payroll as a business expense. And like magic that Two hundred dollars is going to come back to you at tax time.

I have a very good friend named Mark. Mark is a very intelligent man with a very successful business of his own. Mark pays his kids to scan all of his receipts to his computer to prepare for taxes. Mark also has his own app that does this same exact thing. So does Mark need his kids to scan his receipts? No, but it's a benefit towards his taxes. Not only that, but it's a benefit for his kids. He doesn't need them to scan his receipts, I mean the man has his own app that will do it for him. But as a father he needs to teach his kids an important lesson. One we all learn. The lesson of working hard for your money. I also bet since Mark's kids work for their money they're not getting an allowance. So in a twisted sense of thought, Mark is kind of writing off their allowance on his taxes. Which in this case is completely legal because again, their working in his business and they're on his payroll.

There are many things you can write off as a tax deduction, I'd even venture to say if you're creative enough and have a good CPA, there probably isn't much you couldn't write off on your taxes. You just need the right justification for it and a very brave CPA. For example, I have a smartwatch. I write my smartwatch off on my taxes. How can I do this? Simple, my smartwatch helps make me money. I can check my texts, calls, emails on my smartwatch. In my Real Estate business, I can search on popular websites for properties that are for sale. I can set reminders on my watch for meeting I have later in the week. I can do just about everything on my watch that I can on my phone, and my phone is a One Hundred percent tax deduction, so why shouldn't my smartwatch be?

But by far in my experience in the business world I've learned that the best way to pay as little in taxes as possible, with the greatest return, is to own multiple businesses.

For example, I own a Real Estate Investment business, so all of my office supplies, part of my rent, car, utilities, etc. are all tax deductible. My wife owns an entertainment business. Essentially she has created a business around running a YouTube channel. What are some of the things she can write off you might ask? Great question! She can write off video games for one, and let's face it, who wouldn't love to write off video games on their taxes. In some cases, she can even write off trips to special events, such as Comic-Con because she is networking with other YouTubers, building her network therefore building her business and making more money.

Another example would be my car. My car is a One Hundred percent tax deduction. The car payment, gas, mileage, oil changes, windshield wipers, all of it. Because I have magnets on each side of my car telling everyone who sees it that I am a Real Estate Investor and what number they can reach me at. Essentially I'm driving around a mobile billboard. Again it's a business expense therefore it is One Hundred percent tax deductible.

What I would suggest to everyone reading this book is to take a week, go through your normal daily routine, and every time you do something that is helping your business, helping you make money, write it down. After One to Two weeks go through the list of everything you've written down and find a way that you could justifyingly write it off on your taxes. Even if it's only a few dollars you save. One dollar a day for Three Hundred Sixty-Five days adds up. Could you use an extra Three Hundred Sixty-Five dollars? I know I could.

Recap

Look at the world around you, look at your business, everything that lies in between both of those two things should be written off on your taxes to some degree. That's how the wealthy do it, the must be doing it for a reason write?

Many of the things we have in our daily lives we overlook. Things that cost us money, things that help us grow as individuals and as a business. These are all things that the wealthy use to their advantage. You just need to be a little creative.

Secret Number 5

Doing The Deed

What most people don't understand is just how difficult it is being your own boss. Making yourself get out of bed in the morning, shutting the television off, not playing that new game, not going to the pool with your kids just because it's nice outside. This is probably the hardest thing a person can do in this day and age. I even have a difficult time with it some days. You wake up in the morning and tell yourself "It's only one day, I can take the day off, I did quite a bit of work yesterday." But it's not, it's not just one day, believe me when I tell you one day can turn into a week really fast. I know this from personal experience.

There have been plenty of times I've told myself "I'm just going to take today off." I've even told myself "I'll get started in a few hours, I'm tired." And very quickly those few hours or that one day turn into days, maybe a week.

I partially blame this on the school system we currently have. We're raised from an early age "Do what the teacher tells you." "This is due tomorrow." Things of that nature. I mean, can you blame anyone for having such a difficult time working for themselves and wanting to get straight to work? I can't.

But see, the wealthy they've learned to suppress those urges to relax when there is work to be done. In fact now that I've learned this trait, I find myself working longer hours, doing more work, and skipping whatever free time I had set aside for the day. I don't do it on purpose, I do it because over the last few years that little voice in my head that tells me to wait until tomorrow, I've completely muted it. I find work to do, even when I thought there wasn't any. I've even gone over and done the same thing multiple times in one day, even though I didn't really need to. It's just habit now.

This is a necessity to becoming one of the wealthy. It's a necessity for many reasons. One being, you need to get your work done, if you don't do your work, you're not going to get paid and your business will crumble right before your eyes. And two, because the more work you do the more you get paid, which in turn means the more time you can take off to do these fun things without it hindering you financially.

Think of it this way, if my goal for the year is to make Two Hundred and Fifty Thousand Dollars and I work so hard that by November I've already made Three Hundred Thousand Dollars, I think I've earned a little vacation time haven't I? Maybe not two months, but a week or two. Plus, I've earned an extra Fifty Thousand Dollars I hadn't planned on. What could you do with an extra Fifty Thousand Dollars in your pocket? I know what I'd do, I'd take me and my family on a two-week vacation anywhere in the world they wanted to go.

But see you can't do these things if you don't do the deed of working when you're supposed to. Now I'm not saying you need to be working non-stop for ten months out of the year. You know your business and it's needs better than I do. You have to make the decision on how much money you want to make in one year and then work hard enough to earn it.

Doing the deed is what separates the working classes. I know many people think that money or the lack of, separates the working classes but that's just not the case. Anyone can make more money. Just read this book and start a business, as long as you follow these principles you have a much higher chance of making more money than Joe Schmoe in the cubicle down the hall.

What separates the working classes is the ability to do the work that it takes to make more money and become financially free. That's why so many businesses fail and why so few people have found the secret to becoming wealthy. The answer is staring you in the face when you look in the mirror, it's whispering in your ear when you wake up in the morning. You just haven't been told this before. The wealthy know this and believe me when I say the wealthy don't care if you're lazy. As long as you don't work for them. There is only so much money in the world. They can only print off so many One Hundred dollar bills a day. The lazier you are and the more you listen to that little voice in your head telling you to take the day off, the more of that money goes to the wealthy.

Now it may take years for you to become successful and financially free. It may take half your lifetime for you to finally become wealthy, but that is all dependent on one thing.

You.

And I need to say, it's not all just about doing the work. You need to be thinking about work, your business, all the time. Every day you need to think about how you can help automate your business, how you can create more simple systems that have the same or better results. The world of business is an ever changing beast and you need to always be thinking of ways to adapt to those changes.

You don't have to be the smartest person in the room, the luckiest, or even the best dressed. What you need to do above all else is "Do the deed." Without that you will never be successful, you'll never be wealthy, and you'll never be financially free.

But if you do, in time, you will have more money than you will ever need. But more importantly than that, you'll have more time. Because that's what's really important. I don't know about you, but when I'm lying on my deathbed surrounded by my loved ones, I'm not going to want more money. I'm going to want more time, with them. All money is, is the ability to spend more time with your family, your friends, your wife and kids. Whoever you want to spend that time with. So don't work hard for money. Work hard so you can spend more time with your family, so your kids never have to worry about money, so they can spend more time with their loved ones.

Your Key to Success

Your key to success is this book. I hope you've read every word of it. I hope you've soaked up all the information. And I truly hope you follow its guidelines and become financially free.

I may have my beliefs and you have yours but I think there is one thing we all as humans can agree on. We weren't put here to work our entire lives away.

Time is your most powerful currency. You can either trade it to someone else for a dollar amount. Or you can trade it for more time and freedom, for not only yourself, for your family and the next three generations after you.

I hope this book helped and I hope to see you on a beach somewhere so you can tell me all about how you learned The Secrets of the Wealthy.

www.ingramcontent.com/pod-product-compliance
Lightning Source LLC
Chambersburg PA
CBHW070420190526
45169CB00003B/1349